# COLOR
## WITH CONFIDENCE

# YOUR ROOMS, YOUR WAY

Meredith Books
Des Moines, Iowa

*Color with Confidence*
Editor: Amy Tincher-Durik
Project Editor: Wanda J. Ventling
Graphic Designers: Brad Ruppert, Sundie Ruppert (Studio G)
Copy Chief: Terri Fredrickson
Publishing Operations Manager: Karen Schirm
Senior Editor, Asset and Information Manager: Phillip Morgan
Edit and Design Production Coordinator: Mary Lee Gavin
Editorial Assistant: Kaye Chabot
Book Production Managers: Pam Kvitne, Marjorie J. Schenkelberg, Rick von Holdt, Mark Weaver
Contributing Copy Editor: Kelly Roberson
Contributing Proofreaders: Heidi Johnson, Jody Speer, Linda Wagner
Cover Photographers: John Forsman (center), Bob Greenspan (left), Eric Roth (right)
Indexer: Don Gulbrandsen

**Meredith® Books**
Executive Director, Editorial: Gregory H. Kayko
Executive Director, Design: Matt Strelecki
Senior Editor/Group Manager: Vicki Leigh Ingham
Senior Associate Design Director: Mick Schnepf
Marketing Product Manager: Tyler Woods

Publisher and Editor in Chief: James D. Blume
Editorial Director: Linda Raglan Cunningham
Executive Director, New Business Development: Todd M. Davis
Executive Director, Sales: Ken Zagor
Director, Operations: George A. Susral
Director, Production: Douglas M. Johnston
Director, Marketing: Amy Nichols
Business Director: Jim Leonard

Vice President and General Manager: Douglas J. Guendel

*Better Homes and Gardens® Magazine*
Editor in Chief: Karol DeWulf Nickell
Deputy Editor, Home Design: Oma Blaise Ford

**Meredith Publishing Group**
President: Jack Griffin
Executive Vice President: Bob Mate

**Meredith Corporation**
Chairman and Chief Executive Officer: William T. Kerr
President and Chief Operating Officer: Stephen M. Lacy

In Memoriam: E.T. Meredith III (1933–2003)

All of us at Meredith® Books are dedicated to providing you with information and ideas to enhance your home. We welcome your comments and suggestions. Write to us at: Meredith Books, Home Decorating and Design Editorial Department, 1716 Locust St., Des Moines, IA 50309-3023.

If you would like to purchase any of our home decorating and design, cooking, crafts, gardening, or home improvement books, check wherever quality books are sold. Or visit us at: bhgbooks.com

# Contents

# Using Color with Confidence

Break out of the beige doldrums and into a whole new world of color opportunities! This book shows you how adding color can be fun—and add joy and value to your home. The spaces featured throughout this book offer two ways to achieve interior design success: Copy the easy-to-understand looks directly, or use the lessons to inspire your own colorful dream rooms. Either way, you can be sure your choices will be color perfect.

## How to Use This Book

This book is divided into chapters, each featuring a different room of the home. Throughout the book, a band of multiwidth stripes can be found at the top of each page. These stripes reflect the colors used in the rooms on that page and are a quick reference to how the colors work with one another. This band also provides an opportunity for you to see the intensity differences of the colors and to consider possible combinations and percentages of colors for a palette. The band is a helpful tool when moving through each room-specific section. For example, if you love the yellow and blue dining room on one page and want inspiration for your adjoining living room, turn to that chapter and look for the band with one or more of the colors represented in the original band.

The desire to decorate our homes with color and pattern can be traced to the earliest humans. The Paleolithic people used yellow and reddish-brown earth pigments and black derived from carbon to create cave paintings. Though contemporary methods and materials are more sophisticated, the wish to embellish our domestic environment is a basic instinct and serves to stimulate our minds, please our emotions, influence our behavior, and project our sense of taste and style.

Today endless opportunities exist for bringing color into our homes. Our paint selection has never been broader, and wallpaper and other applied treatments and materials offer another world of options. But walls

# BEFORE AND AFTER

**BLAND ROOMS GO FROM BORING TO BEAUTIFUL** when color is used effectively. These real-life makeovers show the power color has to transform cold rooms into visually warm and pleasing spaces. The master bedroom *top left* and *right* is in a small suburban ranch. The owners wanted to incorporate color into their room to make the space feel like an inviting retreat where they could escape together from a busy work and family life. Though the room is colorful, the walls are painted caramel, a neutral hue. The real color punch comes from the upholstered

headboard and the quilted coverlet—easy items to change for a new look. The dining room *bottom left* and *right* is part of a large kitchen in an open floor plan home. The owners wanted a space that invited their family to eat at the table, rather than in the nearby family room. Bold stripes on one wall add interest, while the remaining walls, painted a warm cream, connect with the other rooms. Draperies, a table runner, and newly upholstered chair seats add more color. The large sisal rug, a lighter neutral than the previous floor covering, also brightens the space.

# Vocabulary of Color Terms

ACCENT COLORS: Used to add interest and variety, accent colors are often chosen from the side of the color wheel opposite the dominant color used in the room. Incorporate accent colors in small amounts for pillows, lampshades, and other accessories.

COLOR WHEEL: A device developed by Isaac Newton as he studied light through a prism and realized that the light broke into the 12 colors of the rainbow. The color wheel is the 12 colors set out in circular form so their relationships can be readily understood. It is a handy tool for creating room color palettes.

COOL COLORS: Also called receding colors, they are blue, violet, and green, or other colors with a large percentage of a cool color in the mix. Cool colors can make a room look larger and make surfaces appear to move away from the eye.

HUE: A pure or base color to which neither black nor white has been added. Also used as another term for color.

NEUTRAL COLORS: These range from black to white, including all grays. Neutrals also include off-whites to chocolate brown. Black and white are technically noncolors but are commonly referred to as colors.

PALETTE: A group of colors that is used by an artist or an interior designer or decorator for a particular picture or room scheme.

PRIMARY COLORS: Three pure colors—red, yellow, and blue—that cannot be produced by mixing other colors together. All other colors are derived from these three.

SATURATION: The intensity, purity, or brightness of a color. Saturated colors are the opposite of muted (or grayed) hues.

SHADES: The tones produced by adding black to a hue. Commonly, the word also means colors that have white, gray, or other hues added to them.

TINTS: The tones of a color produced when white is added. Pastels are tints.

TONE: The gradation of color from its weakest to strongest intensity, for example, bluish-white to deep navy.

WARM COLORS: Also called advancing colors, these are reds, yellows, oranges, and apricots. Warm colors appear to bring surfaces closer and make objects look larger.

aren't the only place to use color. Flooring, countertops, common and exotic woods, tile, cabinet hardware, appliances, light fixtures, frosted and stained glass, lampshades and bases, draperies and blinds, upholstery, pillows, artwork, and accessories are additional tools you can use to colorize your home. And don't forget the color impact from organic or live displays created with such elements as shells, rocks, flowers, and aquariums with fish.

But while we have the widest choices ever for personalizing our homes with color, many homeowners become stressed because the selection is too great. As a result, homes commonly wear builder white walls, beige carpet and tile, and neutral kitchens and baths with the idea that color, pattern, and texture will be added later. The goal of this book is to empower you to make and implement wise and satisfying color decisions so you can begin enjoying the many benefits of the right color mix in your home today.

## The Power of Color

Research has shown that using certain colors can actually affect how you feel and behave. For example, red raises blood pressure, stimulates appetite, and creates excitement. Red is associated with passion, energy, anger, confidence, vitality, and drama. Opposing red on the color wheel is green, its complement. Green is associated with relaxation, balance, harmony, rejuvenation, and heart health.

Some colors energize and uplift people; some calm and quiet them. Depending on the goals you have for your room, certain color choices may be better than others. But understand too the influence a color has can be diminished or increased by using a tint or shade. For example, orange may be energizing, but a tint of orange—pale apricot—can be soothing. The effects of color can also be controlled through the amount of a color used, its placement, and how you balance the hue with other colors.

Color can be used to manipulate the way the eye perceives a space. Warm, or advancing, colors come toward the eye and make a space appear smaller and cozier. Cool, or receding, colors move away from the eye and make a space appear larger and airier. Color can be used to highlight architectural features and hide the flaws of a room. For example, if you have cracked

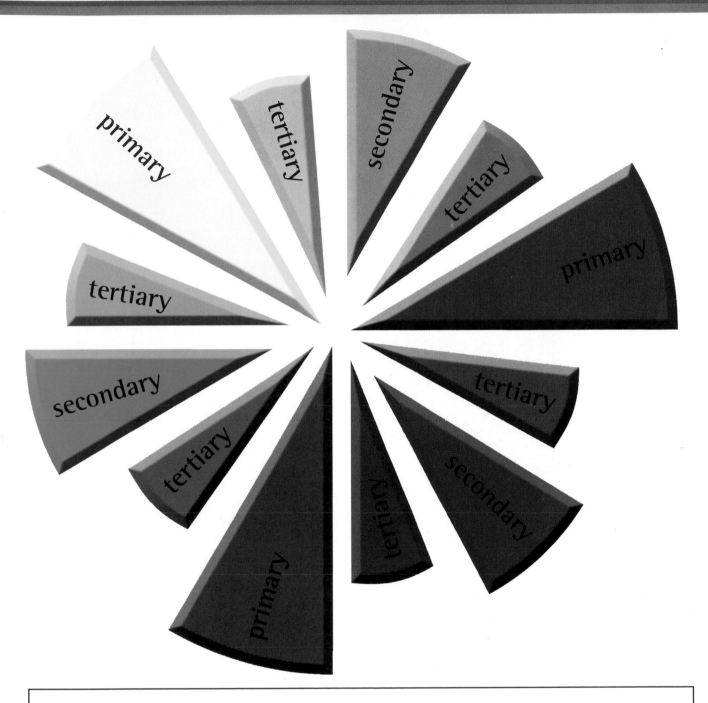

# Using the Color Wheel

THE COLOR WHEEL is divided into three categories: primary, secondary, and tertiary.

THE PRIMARY COLORS are red, yellow, and blue. All other colors come from combining these three colors. When two of the primary colors are mixed, a third color—a secondary color—is created.

THE SECONDARY COLORS are orange, green, and violet. When a primary is mixed with the secondary color next to it, a tertiary color is created.

THERE ARE SIX TERTIARY COLORS: red-orange, red-violet, yellow-green, yellow-orange, blue-green, and blue-violet. Each of these colors can be lightened with white, creating a tint, or deepened with black, creating a shade.

TO MAKE THE PROCESS of selecting colors for your home easier, some sample color schemes and strategies are shown on *pages 10* and *11*. Read about the colors that make up the schemes, then look at the color wheel to explore how many combinations you can devise for your rooms. Use the bands on the top of the pages throughout the book to explore more palette possibilities.

walls in need of repair but a great fireplace, paint the walls a deep, light-absorbing color and the fireplace a light color or white. The shadows caused by the wall cracks will be camouflaged by the intensity of the wall color; the lighter color on the fireplace will force the eye to focus on it, the more attractive feature.

In addition to the psychological and physical benefits of using color, color offers opportunities for self expression. Your home is your haven and the one place where you can be yourself. Choose colors you like living with and establish your home so it looks lived in by you. The right colors will feed your spirit and nurture you and your family and friends for many years.

# SCHEMES

**ANALOGOUS:** A color scheme using adjacent colors, for example, blue, blue-green, and green. Analogous schemes in cool colors are very relaxing, such as in this coastal living room *right*. Warm analogous themes are energized.

**COMPLEMENTARY:** A color scheme using two colors opposite one another on the color wheel, for example, red and green. When these colors are used together, they make each other appear brighter and more intense. In this dining room *middle*, the colors are grayed for a rich appearance.

**MONOCHROMATIC:** A color scheme using a single color and a neutral, for example, the red-and-white living room *above right*. Monochromatic rooms need texture and pattern to make them visually interesting.

**TRIADIC:** A color scheme using three colors, each evenly spaced from the others on the color wheel, for example, red, yellow, and blue. The mix of floral and geometric fabrics in these colors makes this sunroom *far right* a happy space.

ANALOGOUS

COMPLEMENTARY

TRIADIC

# Welcoming Spaces

Public rooms—entryways, living rooms, and dining rooms—greet guests and offer the outside world a first impression of your home. Color plays a vital role in creating an atmosphere and mood in these rooms and can quickly communicate your personality to new visitors. Whether you prefer cool shades of blue to complement your relaxed style or lively fuchsia to show your high energy, if you learn to use color effectively, your home will express your personal style. The spaces on pages 14–45 teach you how to make smart color choices and create a more inviting home.

**RELAXING COMES NATURALLY** in this colorful room *opposite*. Rooms bathed in sunny yellow-green can be too loud for comfort, but neutral-hue furnishings offset the energetic color and make the room feel upbeat, yet appropriate for quiet conversation.

# Living Rooms

Your living room is typically the first room your guests see; use color to give them an accurate impression of your personality. Let the lessons on the following pages help you plan a scheme that reflects who you are, whether you consider yourself playful or serious or you love casual or formal interiors. You'll learn how color can bridge the gap between seemingly different design styles, how to use collections to unify a color scheme, and how to add wow factor to any neutral palette.

## CIRCUS ACT

**COLOR A ROOM HAPPY** with a palette inspired by the costumes of circus performers *left*. A room filled with cotton-candy pink, grape, lemon, and nectarine could be overwhelming, but the hues in this space are grayed for a less imposing appearance. This playful yet grown-up look is achieved by pairing the candy colors with typically serious furniture, including a rolled English-arm sofa, an off-white dainty side table, and cream-color draperies.

# Making Complementary Colors Work for You

You can manipulate complementary colors to create the mood you want. Here are some color combination ideas:

PAIR COMPLEMENTARY COLORS, such as the chartreuse and red in the dining room on *page 36*, for a vivid scheme. Colors that lie opposite each other on the color wheel intensify each other.

IGNITE DRAMA with high-contrast colors. Bold complementaries add zest to an otherwise sedate environment *above*.

For a highly colorful room, use more than one pair of complementaries, such as in the child's room on *page 111*. Use shades and tints to prevent the colors from becoming overwhelming.

USE RELATED HARMONIES, different tones of the same color or side-by-side hues on the color wheel, to add visual interest to a complementary scheme. For example, use different shades of green and yellow with red, such as in the guest room on *page 102*. By limiting the

amount of an accent color, the scheme is more subdued.

MUTE COMPLEMENTARIES with gray for a more subtle palette, such as in the bathroom on *page 122 left*.

NEUTRALIZE BOLD COLORS with white, off-white, taupe, gray, brown, and black, as shown *opposite bottom*. These neutral colors—shown here on the flooring, trim, and accessories—can tone down a potentially overpowering color scheme.

# CITRUS

**BLOOMING COLOR**—lemon, honeydew, watermelon, and poppy—abounds in this living room *opposite*. These vivid hues could easily overwhelm the space, but neutrals, including the white molding, white ceiling, and wood furnishings, provide color relief. Natural light from the tall windows also balances the lively palette.

**SLEEK MID-CENTURY MODERN FURNITURE** in eye-popping colors warms an otherwise cool space *below*. Without these cheerful pieces, the living room's nearly all-white scheme and hard-line architecture could be sterile and uninviting.

**FRAMED ART** *right* offers a great way to establish a multicolor palette in a room reserved for conversation. The white mats and soft wall color allow the artwork to add bursts of color without disrupting the relaxed atmosphere. The red pillows emphasize the red prints.

# SHERBET

**PALE LIME WALLS** freshen the living room *opposite*; combined with the white molding and mantel, the space appears clean and crisp. Dashes of warm pink and orange prevent the room from turning cold. If your room has strong natural light—similar to this space—use it to warm cool colors.

**FROSTY ORANGE SHERBET** walls and artwork pair with white to create a comfy space that invites conversation *right*. Enliven a quiet palette of white and soft hues with green plants and accessories.

**LEMON AND LIME** dominate this space *below*. Because the intensity of the yellow and green tones is similar, the scheme is harmonized, not jarring. Dollops of warm pinks and reds—on the striped chair upholstery, the bold pillow on the sofa, and pretty flowers—break up the otherwise homogenous palette, while black and off-white accents and dark wood tones ground the palette.

**BOLD PINK AND NECTAR** jazz up this sophisticated brown and cream living room *opposite* for a look that's anything but timid. Off-white and coffee create drama; positioned between a pair of grand windows, the bright, oversized painting is an unexpected focal point in the traditional setting.

**VARYING WIDTHS OF STRIPES** (wide on the walls and narrow on the decorative pillows) add visual texture to this neutral-dominant room *below*. The vivid painting is an instant attention grabber; the coral accents in the draperies echo the bold hues in the painting, connecting the elements.

**DETAILS MAKE THE DIFFERENCE** in this living room *left*. Though the space started with a great foundation of white furniture accented with rich brown wood, it's the accessories and their placement—the throw with a Greek key pattern in two shades of chocolate on the tufted bench, the graphic pillow on the white sofa, and the sensuous shell sculpture on a deep brown table—that make the room a success. Together they add interest through changes in color intensity and variety of line.

# HOT CHOCOLATE

# Enliven Mocha with Accents and Textures

Brown is an inviting and easy color to live with, especially when used in large spaces. It can be dark and rich, such as an espresso hue, or tinted with white to become the color of a latte. Use deep browns to make a large space feel more cozy and luxurious and lighter shades to add subtle warmth to small rooms.

ADD SURPRISE to a brown and cream palette with bursts of color. The most dramatic schemes—which pair the darkest browns with the palest creams—can handle bold color accents, such as orange, lipstick red, and chartreuse. More subtle palettes, such as milk chocolate and cream, are made more charming with the addition of less-

intense colors, including sky blue, lilac, powder pink, apricot, and moss green.

CHANGE THE MIX of a space that's dominated by neutrals whenever the mood strikes—without interrupting the foundation. Because accent colors can be isolated to small accessories, artwork, or decorative textiles (such as pillows and throws) in an all-neutral room, it's easy to change them on a whim or for the season.

USE VISUAL AND TOUCHABLE TEXTURE to add interest—and well-placed color—in a room with a neutral color scheme. To excite the senses, place soft, fuzzy pillows—such as

the round brown pillows *above*—on tightly woven neutral-tone furnishings.

PLAY WITH SCALE by using oversize accessories for drama. For example, the white brackets and urns on either side of the mirror *above* contrast with the deep brown walls, but it's the scale of these objects that adds interest to the wall.

METALLIC FINISHES AND MIRRORS add sparkle and depth to rooms with near-monochromatic schemes. These elements can magnify accent colors used throughout a space or bring focal-point status to colorful accessories (such as a sparkly frame around bright artwork in an all-neutral room).

# WATERCOLORS

**ROSY PINKS** add warmth to a cool blue and white room *above* and *opposite*. Other happy colors, such as apricot, buttercream, and burnt orange, can also warm up a serene scheme. Change the look of a space by introducing accents—such as flowers—in colors that reflect the season (soft tones in the spring and deeper tones in the winter).

**CLUSTERS OF COLLECTIONS** create greater drama than an individual item can offer, especially when the color is pale. The pottery vases in earthy tans and blues *above right* compose a still life; the shapes and subtle color changes of the vases are enhanced by natural shadows, which give the grouping importance.

**BIG BLUE ACCENTS** act as a link between the eclectic furnishings and accessories in this living room *right*. The grand scale of the objects—the oversize globe and coffee table—and deep intensity of the blues increase the drama of the room.

**COOL POWDER BLUE WASHES** the walls with pretty color *opposite*. Add warmth to chilly hues with natural-fiber rugs and fabrics and distressed furniture. Here the original wood finish of the table and bowl peeks through a chipped white overcoat.

# VARIATIONS ON WHITE

**WHITE-ON-WHITE** is an elegant color palette, as the living room *opposite* proves. The keys to making this monochromatic palette interesting are diversity of tones— from deeper shades to lighter tints—as well as texture and pattern. When selecting paint, upholstery, flooring, draperies, and accessories, include a range of whites, from pure and cool to creamy and warm. Add interest to the palette by incorporating white-on-white patterns and using contrasting textures, such as the soft cashmere throw resting on the tightly woven upholstery of the chair.

**A WHITE FOUNDATION** fades into the background and places importance on the colorful art and pillows in the space *right*. Because white plays a supporting role—the bold artwork and pillows create a focal point—the textural and intensity changes of the color are less important. The black coffee table grounds the furniture arrangement.

**A WARM-WHITE SOFA** supports a trio of pillows in golden hues *below*, showing how white can be very inviting, even in cold climates. The sense of coziness in this living room is amplified with the addition of textural elements and warm tones: the natural rug, napped-fiber upholstery, and wood accents.

# Foyers and Entries

Color is the key to creating an eye-catching, personality-filled entryway. Warm tones, such as sunny yellows and rich reds, are friendly and welcoming, but cool colors, including greens and blues, and peaceful neutrals promote instant relaxation. The examples on the following pages prove both warm and cool palettes make a great first impression.

## STOP AND SMELL THE ROSES

**COLORS PLUCKED FROM A SPRING GARDEN** welcome guests to a modern country home *opposite*. Azalea-pink walls offer an inviting first impression. White trim and natural light from the sidelights neutralize the boldness of the dominant pink hue and give the space a clean look. To relax this entryway and achieve a country aesthetic, a deeper-tone cool color, hyacinth-blue, covers the door. The dark wood flooring and deep blue door provide visual weight to ground the space.

**ROSE-COLORED WALLS** and leisure-time accents make this entryway *right* a joy to pass through for family and guests. The accessories play an important role in the success of the space: The fishing gear, hats, fish plaques, and outerwear in aged neutrals, browns, and greens take the edge off the red-tone walls. In addition, a touch of black—on the fishing poles and the binoculars—further prevents the red from being overly sweet and syrupy. White adds a fresh, clean feel, while the rich wood flooring, door, and trunk further the country feel and visually ground the palette.

# GREENS AND YELLOWS

**ELECTRIC LEMONGRASS**, a green-yellow hue, vibrates against its complement, red (in the undertones of the wood credenza) *opposite*. This edgy palette, along with the sleek furniture and black architectural lamps, gives this entryway an urban buzz. Turn down the temperature on an energized palette by introducing accents in cool aqua, sky blue, and green—as the oversize poster and vase do here.

**TWO-TONE YELLOW WALLS**—a pale yellow background with vivid golden accents—offer a fresh-faced welcome *below*. A touch of gray-blue in the curvy hand-painted chair rail adds subtle contrast to the sunny palette.

**GREENS WITH BLUE AND YELLOW UNDERTONES** are mottled on with rags for a nature-inspired wall that is easy on the senses *right*. Use fresh flowers and plants or accessories with organic shapes to bring life into similar calming spaces.

# BLUE SKIES

**COOL GRAY-BLUE WALLS** recede into the background and allow the rich woods *left* to take center stage. To make a stormy-weather blue such as this work in a space that receives little sunlight, add some heat with healthy doses of reds and chocolate browns. Here the wood patinas, faded-rose accents on the carpet runner, and red picture matting warm up the entry and hallway.

**COLOR IT EASY** with a monochromatic carpet runner for entryway stairs. This jaunty runner—with a pale to dark blue and white stripe pattern—*above* suits this seaside house perfectly and adds color without having to paint the tall stairwell walls (not shown).

**BREATHE LIFE INTO** deep blue walls with bold accents in complementary and warm colors, as the orange flowers and lemons do in this entryway *opposite*. Without punches of color, this space would be boring and sedate.

# PEACEFUL INTERLUDES

**CONCRETE SLABS CURVE GRACEFULLY** to form a sanctum just inside the front door of this contemporary home *left*. Often, gray concrete is too cold and uninviting for a home entryway, but the wash of warm light on the creamy-tone artwork and the richly grained wood floor make the space both interesting and welcoming.

**THE SHADES OF COCOA** used in this entryway *below* nurture the soul like a cup of hot chocolate soothes the body. When selecting palettes for your home, consider color associations like this to elicit the response you want. But have plenty of food and beverage on hand when guests come calling—especially when you select rich browns that make them think of chocolate and coffee!

**ALTER YOUR MOOD** after a stressful day by creating a serene still life in your entry. This quiet scene *opposite* is washed in earthy and watery hues—and the artwork speaks of a tranquil getaway—promoting an instant sense of calm.

# Let Local Color Influence Your Entryway

WHAT'S OUTSIDE YOUR HOME? The colors that appear in your neighborhood can influence your interior palette: You can either mimic the outside world or create an environment that contrasts with your surroundings. For instance, if you live in a subdivision where the exterior choices are limited to grayed earth tones, you can continue the palette in the entry of your home to prevent a jarring contrast—or choose a wildly different scheme to break up the monotony.

MAXIMIZE LOCAL COLOR If you love the colors of your area, repeat them inside. If you live by the ocean, for example, a selection of watery blues and sandy taupes can be very pleasing. In a neighborhood of brightly painted Victorians, use some of those colors as accents in your entry. The repetition of neighborhood color, even in small amounts, will connect your interior to the outside world. The result will be a smooth transition from outside in, offering a sense of community.

MINIMIZE LOCAL COLOR If the outside world is stressful, use your entryway as a chef uses a palate cleanser: Neutralize the effects with opposites. For example, if your surroundings contain too much color, use cool, grayed tones to relax your interior. Is the outside too bland? Energize your interiors with warm colors, such as bold pinks, reds, or oranges.

# Dining Rooms

In today's hurried world, sharing a meal with friends and family is an experience to be savored, especially when all the senses are treated with care. Of course, great food and good conversation are imperative to a pleasant meal, but the room in which the meal is served also plays an important role. Use the color lessons from the spaces on the following pages to help you create a dining room that offers a visually appealing and soul-nourishing ambience.

## SEEING RED

**RED STIMULATES THE APPETITE** and encourages conversation; the dining room *opposite* achieves both objectives with its bold walls. Select a red with blue or brown undertones to prevent red walls from appearing too intense, which can make white linens and molding look dingy and visually reduce the size of your room. To break up large expanses of a bold red, incorporate large furnishings or artwork, as shown in this dining room.

**WALLS UPHOLSTERED IN RED AND WHITE GINGHAM** create a cozy dining room with cheerful country flair *right*. Neutral-tone elements, such as the sisal rug and the honey-hue table and chairs, and the pale yellow floral upholstery soften the intense palette and busy check pattern. Black accents—including the side table and chandelier—ground the bold scheme. The black frames and white mats promote the botanical prints as focal points.

IF YOU LOVE trendy colors but are afraid of committing to hues that may soon be out of fashion, use them for furnishings that can easily be disguised. If the owner of the dining room *opposite* tires of the rosy-red chairs against the chartreuse walls, for example, the chairs can easily be slipcovered.

EXPAND A COLOR PALETTE by adding accents with flowers or seasonal decorations. The fall bouquet *left* complements the dominant color—red—but enlivens the space with fresh greens and yellows.

USE A WHITE FOUNDATION to lessen the effects of dramatic color combinations, such as red and green *below*. The hues are saturated, but because they are used in small doses—including the red-patterned wallpaper and fresh greenery—they don't overpower the space.

## WARM AND INVITING

# TWIST ON LIME

**PALE GREEN WALLS** provide a clean, restful backdrop for ornate furnishings and a black-and-white-patterned carpet *above*. Golden accents and warm-white linen chair upholstery warm the cool palette, making it friendlier.

**A WALL-SPANNING SILK SCREEN** and floral slipcovers with green accents enliven a neutral room *right*. Elements that are easy to install and remove, including artwork and fabric accents, offer a simple way to introduce color to spaces where changing paint and wallpaper are not possible, such as in rental homes and apartments.

**TOGETHER, LIME AND DELFT BLUE** *opposite* jazz up a quiet interior. The two lively hues are present in equal amounts, so neither overpowers the space. The fun colors and mix of patterns add a bright and casual note to the deep brown-black wood grains of the table and hutch, the sisal flooring, and the neutral-tone walls.

**A VARIETY OF NEUTRALS**—from warm white to deep chocolate—prevents the color scheme in this dining room *left* from being dull. The mix of textures, from the shiny tablecloth to the velvety upholstery and rugged chandelier, adds visual, touchable interest.

**BROWN FABRIC ON CANVAS STRETCHERS** *below* creates a dramatic focal point against the café-au-lait-hue walls. Artwork such as this is both a sophisticated and an inexpensive way to add impact to any space. The strategic placement also accentuates the best features of the chandelier: the crystals and graceful lines.

**COFFEE-BEAN BROWN AND CREAM** are in the same color family (brown), but they are high-contrast hues: The coffee-bean color is deepened with black, while the cream hue is lightened with white. Pairing the two creates drama, as this elegant dining room *opposite* proves. The furnishings and accessories provide unity between the colors: The chair upholstery mixes cream and a midtone brown, while the curtain panel features all three hues.

# COFFEE WITH CREAM

# SUNNY SKIES

**BRIGHT YELLOW** pairs with white to create a sunny space in which to dine and enjoy conversation *left*. By limiting the palette to one color and using white sparingly to break up the expanses of bold color, the graphic elements—such as the wall stripes and the curved chair back—are easier to distinguish. This use of graphic shapes was common in home interiors in the 1960s and early 1970s and is gaining popularity today.

**ONE SHADE OF BLUE** combines with white beaded board, ironstone dinnerware, and farmhouse furnishings to create a friendly country atmosphere *below*. The powdery blue, which recedes into the background, leads the eye to the focal-point painting.

**ROOMS WITH A BLACK AND WHITE PALETTE,** such as the dining space *opposite*, can be cold and uninviting, but the addition of one strong color—in this case a saturated yellow—in small doses is enough to counter the black and warm the space.

# Use Color to Manipulate Architecture

Color can play an important role in showcasing strong architecture, disguising problems, and creating interest when the architecture has little character. Use these ideas to make the most of the structural elements in your dining room or any room of the home:

TOO-LARGE OR VACANT-FEELING ROOMS look best in dark or warm colors, including chocolate brown or russet, which make a space feel cozy. These colors also help make a skimpily furnished room feel well-appointed.

TOO-SMALL ROOMS are visually expanded with light, airy colors, such as pale blue and lilac. Keep the intensity of the floor and ceiling the same as the walls to create the most impact.

LOW CEILINGS, when painted in pale tints or neutrals, recede, making the ceilings appear higher.

HIGH CEILINGS that make a room feel cavernous can be lowered visually with warm colors, which appear to advance.

ROOMS THAT RECEIVE little natural light are more appealing in happy colors, such as peony pink, apple green, and lemon yellow. These colors are especially uplifting and energizing when paired with white. Because these colors reflect light, paint them only on walls that are in good repair. For walls with flaws, use a heavyweight, patterned wallcovering or a mottled paint treatment.

CRACKED OR DAMAGED WALLS look best when painted with dark or warm colors; these colors absorb light, which helps hide imperfections.

ROOMS LACKING A FOCAL POINT gain one when a single wall is painted a bold or contrasting color. Placing art on a wall further draws the eye to this feature.

ROOMS WITH TOO MANY FEATURES become visually calmer when painted the same light-intensity neutral.

# Sources of Color Inspiration

Ideas for dining room color palettes are everywhere. Here are a few places you can find color combinations that work for eating and entertaining spaces, as well as for the rest of your home. Once you find the right colors for your space, select paint cards that match the chosen hues and carry them with you whenever you shop. *Note: Use a three-ring binder as a design notebook to store paint cards and fabric swatches. Fill the binder with plastic sleeves to hold samples, and use dividers to separate the materials for each room.*

MAGAZINES AND BOOKS are excellent sources for examples of rooms decorated in myriad styles and color palettes.

YOUR CLOSET can provide clues to personal color preferences. Clothing accessories, such as scarves and ties, often contain color groupings that can be adapted for room settings.

NATURE OFFERS many successful color combinations. For instance, study the intricate colorations in a piece of

limestone or a leaf for monochromatic palettes. Or look to a beach, forest, meadow, or the mountains for other natural combinations that will translate well into your home.

FRUITS AND VEGETABLES are the colors of nature's bounty. Arrange fruits and veggies to find fun schemes.

COLLECTIONS—dishes, pottery, quilts, globes, and art—displayed in the room can provide color inspiration.

# PASTELS

**APRICOT WALLS** *opposite* could set the stage for an overly sweet space, but this sugary color is balanced by cool green—fresh plants and the oversize rug motif—and white—the casually draped tablecloth, trim, and ceiling—for a relaxed feel. Foliage—fresh, dried, or artificial—enlivens both warm and neutral settings.

**WIDE PINK AND WHITE STRIPES** on the chairs and oversize lilac and white floor tiles make this dining room *right* pretty enough for a princess. The wood tabletop offers visual weight, while the white walls and trim keep the focus on the patterns.

**TO PRESERVE THE FORMAL FEEL** of an all-white space, add quiet color in limited doses—such as the pale teal draperies in this dining room *below*. Though this space has a very cool palette, it is inviting rather than cold due to the abundance of richly grained wood furniture.

# Gathering Spaces

Bring family and friends together in a joy-filled space designed for relaxed entertaining. Great-rooms (a family or living room/kitchen combo), family rooms, sunrooms, and home theaters are all natural spaces in which to spend time with and entertain those most dear. This section shows you how to create the right look for each of these unique rooms, whether it's to be used for a sunny respite, a convivial evening among friends, or a movie with the kids.

RESTFUL COLORS and easy-care leather and rattan furniture make this family room *opposite* inviting. Because the yellow wall color is grayed—and not too bright—it enhances the warm, welcoming atmosphere.

# Great-Rooms

Whether it's a place to unwrap gifts by the fire, a spot to share a cup of coffee with a friend, or a play area for kids, great-rooms and family rooms need to be stylish and durable. Color is key, especially for unifying a great-room, which—because of the adjoining kitchen and dining area—can be more disjointed than a single-purpose family room. The following pages show how color can add continuity and comfort to these rooms.

## POWER OF RED

USE RED TO CREATE A COZY ENVIRONMENT in a large great-room. To prevent red walls from overpowering a space, select a color with a blue undertone—similar to the shade shown *left*; the blue cools down the red, making the color easier to live with. The stone fireplace, neutral-tone furnishings, and white trim also reduce the harshness of the bold walls. Red is a good color for the nearby eating and kitchen areas (not shown) because it encourages the appetite.

# Create Color Continuity in an Open Space

Color is a powerful tool for transforming a plain room with an open floor plan into a sensational space. The following tips will help you determine how and where to use color to define a space.

**CEILINGS:** White is a fail-safe ceiling color, but you have other options: If your room has strong natural light and a high ceiling, you can use a low-intensity color for the ceiling and walls, as shown *above*. Because the yellow in this family room is light and bright—and it is paired with light-color flooring and white trim—the space feels airy, not claustrophobic. If the wall colors are intense, select a soft neutral hue or a pale tint of the wall color for the ceiling.

**FLOORS:** Great-rooms can be divided into separate areas with flooring changes, for example, carpet for the sitting area and tile for the kitchen. Rugs can further define the areas: The dining area might be grounded with a sisal rug, while the furniture grouping in the living room is unified by a multicolor area rug.

**WALLS:** Color can fill entire planes in an open floor plan (floor to ceiling and corner to corner), as shown in the two-story great-room *opposite left*. However, color also can be used to define functional areas within a space—such as a play area—or call attention to important details (for instance, to highlight a focal-point wall or

architectural detail). If you plan to use wall color to create zones within a great-room, choose colors with a similar intensity to make a seamless transition between the areas.

**TRIM:** For visual continuity, use the same color or finish of trim in a great-room. A combination of wood and painted trim offers pleasing contrast—as the space *opposite right* and on *page 54* proves—but achieving the right balance can be tricky. To experiment with various options, sketch all the elements of your room in an elevation (side view); color the trim and other architectural details to audition the placement of painted and/or light and dark wood tones.

# SUNNY SIDE

**FRESH LEMON** walls brighten this family room *opposite* as well as the spirits of those who spend time there. If you live in a cold or rainy climate, select cheery hues like this for rooms in which you gather with family or friends; the happy hues will raise your spirits on dark, gloomy days.

**GOLDENROD—**a deep yellow—partners with a stone fireplace to make this soaring space *left* feel cozier. The plush furnishings in rich red upholstery and reddish wood tones throughout the space further promote a sense of warmth and invite conversation.

**IF YOU LOVE YELLOW** and want a sophisticated yet relaxed space, follow the cues in this family room *below*. The combination of walnut-stained beams and bookshelves, carved pilasters with capstones, and dark-stained, ornate furniture brings architectural interest and grounds the lighthearted daisy-yellow color. Though this room is more formal than most family rooms, its relaxed elements—the English garden-print floral fabric, makeshift coffee table, and pottery—create an intimate sitting room.

# GREAT GREENS

**BRIGHT, FRESH YELLOW–GREEN** makes a successful transition between the living and dining areas in this great-room *above* because of the continuity of the white trim. The wall color gives the overstuffed blue-green sofa an updated look (typical taupe walls would have made the sofa look like yesterday's news).

**PARK–BENCH GREEN** *right* evokes memories of lush lawns and lazy summer days. In this great-room, the dark color conceals unsightly vents and reduces the visual noise of colorful books. To intensify a deep color such as this, incorporate some elements in the complementary color (here a red sofa and warm-tone, outdoor-inspired furnishings do just that).

**OLIVE GREEN ACCENTS,** ranging from the light wall color to the dark chair upholstery, unify this great-room *opposite*. The greens in this room are in the same color family (the chairs are a deeper shade of the wall color). To create a similar cohesive color scheme, select the hues for various elements in the room—walls, fabrics, rugs, accessories—from one gradated paint strip.

# PEACEFUL BLUES

**BRING COLOR INTO A NEUTRAL ROOM** with textiles. Soothing blue and soft yellow—in the upholstery, pillows, and decorative accessories—offer a bounty of color in this great-room *left* without detracting from the stunning views from the wall of windows. In a room with less exciting scenery, mix very pale and deeper blues to create the drama.

**ACCENTS,** such as this blue throw *above*, offer an easy, inexpensive way to introduce seasonal color in a great-room or family room. Small accessories and textiles—place mats on a table, a cluster of candles on a mantel, an area rug, and new slipcovers for existing throw pillows—disperse fresh color without significant changes to wall color or flooring.

# NATURAL DRAMA

**HIGH–CONTRAST COLOR SCHEMES** increase the drama of any space. This great-room *right* features a powerful contrasting pair: black and white. Though such contrasting schemes can make a room cold and uninviting, this room welcomes conversation due to the addition of organic elements, including the warm-tone wood treatment on the fireplace, the leaf-color pillows in interesting shapes, and the nature-inspired motif of the rug.

**KEEP THE FOCUS** on important architectural features—such as this limestone fireplace facade *below*—by enveloping them with soft colors. The neutral scheme in this great-room promotes relaxation and quiet conversation. To prevent an all-neutral room from being too sedate, incorporate small doses of accent colors derived from nature—such as the gemstone-hue chest, pillows, vase, and chair.

# Sunrooms

If you have a sunroom, you have the instant ability to bring the outside in with garden-inspired colors. These cheerful hues—warm yellow, zesty orange, spring green, and summer-sky blue—have the power to brighten your mood on even the dreariest days. The spaces on the following pages show you how to use Mother Nature's palette to create your very own place in the sun. (And, if you don't have a sunroom, follow our tips to bring a sunny outlook to any space of your home.)

## SUN-KISSED YELLOWS

**THE COLOR OF SUNSHINE** is an appropriate choice for a sunroom, and you have myriad options from which to choose—from intense and bright to soft and pale. The uplifting hue in this sunroom *opposite* is a tint of true yellow (white added to the color) grounded by the terra-cotta flooring and earthy brown sofa. If you have views of a wooded lot or lush gardens, choose a similar yellow; paired with white molding, this hue accentuates the scenery.

**BUTTER YELLOW** *right* is a quiet alternative to tart lemon yellows, yet sunnier than golden yellows, which may appear too gloomy. The yellow in this sun-filled room has a hint of red, which warms the color and connects the hue to the red door and warm-tone wood, tile, and pots. Green plants and blue accents prevent the space from getting too warm.

# FRESH PICKS

**TANGY COLOR ABOUNDS** in this sunroom *below*. The bold cabana stripes on the oversize ottoman and bright floral-motif window treatments provide the energy; the remaining upholstered pieces, while vivid, play a subdued supporting role. The white lampshades, black lamp bases, and light-tone flooring balance the bold hues.

**BUILD A PLAYFUL PALETTE** in your sunroom by mixing patterns that share hues. In this space *right*, gingham, stripes, and floral motifs—in pinks, oranges, yellows, blues, and greens—make a cheerful statement rather than overwhelm. The patterns are spread throughout the space and are tempered with large planes of solid colors, including the gray rug and sheer white window coverings.

**EQUAL DOSES** of fruity green, pink, and orange are mixed in this sunroom *opposite* for a tropical look. The ottoman combines all the colors to unify the bold scheme; the white elements give the eye some visual relief.

# Creating a Home Color Palette

To manage color in your home for a cohesive aesthetic that isn't contrived, create a design notebook in which to store plans and swatches and audition new colors (see page 44 for more information). Follow these steps to create your home color palette:

DRAW A PLAN of your home that shows all the rooms and hallways.

INVENTORY what will be in each room, such as the carpet, wall colors, furniture, art, and accessories. Gather swatches or paint chips that represent the colors of these items.

ASSESS THE ROOMS for both positive and negative attributes; note these items. Determine focal points from the list of positive attributes, such as a view, fireplace, or beautiful armoire.

PLAN A STRATEGY using this information: Consider how one room will flow into the next, what mood you want, and the existing items to be incorporated into the color palette.

CREATE THE DESIRED LOOK using the schemes shown throughout this book. Start with a plan for the public rooms, such as the entryway or living room, then move through the house one room at a time. Use gradated paint strips for the palettes; the tints and shades on each strip offer additional choices in varying percentages that can be used for adjoining rooms. For example, the living room may be predominately cocoa and cream with bold pink and orange accents, and the dining room may be shell pink with coral and cream accents.

# RESTFUL HUES

**A MIX OF COOL HUES**—sky-blue walls and furnishings dressed in a springlike bouquet of violet, blue, and green—promotes relaxed living in this sunroom *left*. Furnishings in traditional shapes may seem too sophisticated for such a low-key setting, but the variety of floral upholstery and unmatched stained and painted wood pieces reduces the formality. Keeping all the upholstered elements in the same palette prevents the patterns from being too busy.

**COOL SAGE GREEN** and white create a tranquil setting in this light-filled sunroom *above*. This quiet palette visually turns down the heat in rooms that become too hot during the day.

# Home Theaters

Pop the corn and dim the lights—the show is about to begin! Home theaters are becoming popular additions to many houses, but because of their special light level and acoustic needs, it can be challenging to choose a decorating theme and color scheme. Use the ideas on pages 64–67 to glean inspiration for your own theater—or wherever you watch movies in your home.

## MOCHA AND RED

**RICH BROWNS AND DEEP BRONZES** cause the walls to recede into the background in this home theater *opposite*, placing the spotlight on the main event, the grandly scaled, carved wall unit that holds an oversize television (not shown). Color for home theaters should be light absorbing and have a relatively dark intensity. Accents, such as the red-painted tin-ceiling tiles, add just the right amount of drama when the lights come up.

**DEEP AND MUTED TONES** are the most popular hues for home theaters, and the surfaces in this space *opposite* successfully mix deep green, steel blue, and gray. The curvy panels on the walls and ceiling—which mimic the lines of the chair backs—benefit the room's acoustics.

**WHEN CHOOSING PAINT** for a home theater, opt for a flat finish, which was used for the regal purple walls in this room *left*. This no-sheen finish absorbs light and reduces glare from the big screen.

**TEAL WALLS** offer the only splashes of color in this home theater *below*. The teal hue recedes, putting the emphasis on the warm-tone pillars that surround the television.

# PLUM AND TEAL

# Working Spaces

You likely spend a great deal of time in the hardworking spaces of your home: the home office, kitchen, and laundry room. As such, these are ideal places in which to express your personality through color. Home centers, catalogs, and online sources abound with an ever-increasing array of workspace products—from washable paint and wallpaper to cabinetry, tiles, flooring, and specialty hardware in every color imaginable—sure to capture any mood you desire. The rooms on the following pages prove that a combination of the right elements will make the spaces in which you compute, cook, and clean attractive and functional.

**IF YOU NEED MOTIVATION** in your workspace, introduce high-energy red. In this small home office *opposite*, tomato red is paired with its complement, green, which heightens the effects of the red against the clean white background.

# Kitchens

Great food tastes even better when it's prepared in a kitchen that appeals to all the senses. Kitchens are often referred to as the heart of the home: Besides a place to cook, they are a natural gathering spot for family and friends. Let your personality shine—and encourage the appetite and conversation—by selecting the right hues for every surface. The kitchens on pages 70–79 show you how to use color as a recipe for success.

## HOT AND SPICY

**TOMATO RED** is a terrific color for a kitchen: The warm hue stimulates the palate and is an appealing background for many foods. This commercial-looking kitchen *opposite* feels cozy, thanks to the red on the lower two-thirds of the walls. A strategic use of color—in this instance, using a lighter orange hue to soar to the ceiling—allows you to control the impact of any high-energy hue.

**RED-PAINTED CABINETS** promote a country aesthetic in this kitchen *right*. To prevent the bold color from overpowering the space, the doors of the upper cabinets have patterned-glass inserts; the lower solid-door cabinets ground the scheme. The soft wall color provides further relief from the rich red.

# FRESH FRUIT

**TO HIGHLIGHT A VIVID COLLECTION** of dishware—such as the Fiestaware in this kitchen *left*—choose a low-intensity, contrasting background color to keep the focus on the display. (This technique can be used when showcasing items in any room of the home.) In this space, white and soft yellow provide a quiet backdrop for the dinnerware; the brightly colored prints stand out against the deep blue near the ceiling line.

**A LIMITED PALETTE**—of tomato red and neutrals—shows its serious side in this kitchen *above*, with traditional-style cabinets and hardware. A range of neutrals, from bright white to soft taupe, adds variety to the scheme; dollops of black visually ground the room.

# GARDEN GREENS

**GREEN IS A CALMING COLOR** that works well for rooms with open floor plans. The yellow-green in this space *above* offers a perfect opportunity to bring the outdoors in. White accents "pop" against the contrasting wood tones, which ground the airy scheme.

**IF YOU HAVE A GALLEY KITCHEN,** use color and pattern to visually expand the space. The green and white tile floor in this kitchen *right* is placed on-point to make the space appear wider.

**MUSTARD YELLOW AND GREENS** *opposite* are fresh and cheerful when paired with terra-cotta, white, and warm wood accents. The white island, ceiling beams, and trim add color relief to the bold kitchen.

# Light Your Colors Right

Light—both natural and artificial—impacts the way in which color appears. A combination of light sources and types often is the best solution for meeting functional and aesthetic goals. When selecting colors for your kitchen or any room of your home, keep the following guidelines in mind.

DAYLIGHT is the most pure light source. It offers the truest view of a color and is considered to be the best light in which to make color decisions. Note, though, that color can read differently as the sun moves to various positions in the sky. Throughout the day, the tint of light changes: In the morning, light is clear and bright; in the evening, as the sky

darkens, the light inside is cast with lavender. Seasonal changes also cast different light, from the golden glow of summer to the whiter light of winter.

INCANDESCENT BULBS, which have tungsten filaments, are the most common residential light source. The light from an incandescent bulb has a warmer, yellower cast than natural light. Incandescent lighting is a sound choice for interiors because it doesn't alter color relationships and provides good tonal contrasts.

HALOGEN BULBS also illuminate color relationships and tonal contrasts well, but they offer a whiter and brighter light than incandescent bulbs. Because light

from halogen bulbs appears to sparkle, it is especially good for uplights, downlights, spots, and accent lights. The natural characteristics of halogen light can be used to highlight architectural features or simply enhance interior design with lighting diversity.

FLUORESCENT LIGHTING has the advantage of being the most efficient and longest-lasting artificial light—which is why it is typically used in office buildings—but it tends to cast a greenish light. However, some newer fluorescent bulbs offer brighter, more even lighting that mimics daylight, making this option more appealing for in-home use.

# BLUE RIBBON

**THE DEEP BLUE ISLAND** *opposite*—surrounded by a red and white hand-painted "rug"—is the center of attention, and activity, in this kitchen. The island grounds the soaring sky-blue walls and white cabinets. Red accents dotting the space add visual heat to the cool palette.

**USE A DEEP COLOR** to make a large space more intimate. The upper and lower cabinets *above*, which cover a majority of the wall space, are painted a rich blue, which envelops the room with cozy comfort. If you want to make a small kitchen live larger, use different tones—such as a rich blue on the bottom cabinets and a lighter blue or white on the upper cabinets—to visually expand the space.

**SOME COLORS** have a natural affinity with certain decorating styles. Gray-blue, shown in this kitchen *right*, is a popular choice for country and colonial-style interiors. The cool color gets a warm-up from midtone wood and sunny yellow accents. If you prefer more drama, introduce elements in contrasting colors, such as deep wood tones, black, and orange (the complement of blue).

# NEUTRAL CANVAS

**A NEUTRAL-TONE FINISH** on the furniture-grade cabinetry allows the carved details to take center stage in this kitchen *right*. The bowl of fruit and the niche's mosaic tile pattern offer small doses of color; the deep-tone granite on the island grounds the light scheme. This limited use of color keeps the focus on the craftsmanship.

**ALL-WHITE KITCHENS** offer a blank canvas on which you can add any accent color. In this kitchen *below*, the exposed ceiling beams, walnut-stained floor, and barstools create a modern country aesthetic. Black accents—the cabinet hardware and veins in the marble countertops—punctuate the color scheme.

**CONTEMPORARY, INDUSTRIAL KITCHENS** needn't appear harsh and cold. Weathered wood cabinets offer rugged good looks and offset the stainless-steel appliances in the kitchen *opposite*. Countertop items—including small appliances and cookbooks—supply shots of warm color.

# Home Offices

Whether your home office is a dedicated room or tucked away in the corner of your bedroom, it needs to be an attractive place that encourages healthy work habits. Creating a comfortable, functional office with adequate lighting, inviting furnishings, and a smart layout will help you achieve that goal; use color to establish the environment—energizing or calming—you crave. The spaces on pages 80–85 will show you how to use color effectively in your home office.

## REDS AND BROWNS

**IF YOU TEND TO PROCRASTINATE** and need some incentive to get moving, paint your office red. This passionate color stimulates the brain and emotions, promoting creative work flow. Big doses of white—the flooring, shelves, and trim—in this office *opposite* balance the energizing effects of the bold hue and give the eye a place to rest.

**CHOCOLATE BROWN** fades into the background *right*, ensuring users concentrate on the task at hand rather than the scenery. The combination of deep brown walls and creamy white furnishings and accessories wraps the office in elegance, making this hardworking room feel like a luxury retreat.

# CALM AND COLLECTED

**IF YOU NEED** a restful work environment, select cool colors. To prevent a room with a cool scheme from inducing sleep, introduce neutral or warm tones. The office *above* successfully mixes deep slate green and dark wood tones for a look that's all business. The large painting is a striking focal point on the boldly striped wall.

**FOR A SERENE SPACE** in which to sort mail or file papers, opt for soft neutrals. This workspace *right* encourages quiet with its milk and honey tones.

**SOFT BLUE AND WHITE** and ornate furnishings make this office *opposite* a dreamy place in which to jot a letter. Pink and apricot accents warm up the scheme.

# Alter Your Mood with Color

Research has shown that color can affect an individual's behavior and mood. The following list explains typical human responses to colors. Keep this information in mind as you select colors for your home office or any room—remembering that your response to a particular color may be different from "the norm" due to your personal experiences.

**RED:** This intense, passionate color stimulates the appetite, making it an excellent color for kitchens and dining areas. Pinks promote happiness.

**ORANGE:** A color that is most commonly associated with fruit, orange evokes feelings of warmth, contentment, and wholesomeness. Orange can be cheerful and festive, but large quantities of a bright orange may be overwhelming.

**YELLOW:** The color of the sun, yellow is uplifting and cheery. However, in its pure, bright form, an overabundance of yellow can cause eye fatigue and speed the metabolism.

**GREEN:** Green is the color of calm and rejuvenation; studies have shown that this hue has a neutralizing effect on the nervous system. Green can take many forms, from soft, peaceful tints to deep, dark shades.

**BLUE:** Blue represents wisdom, trust, and peace. This calming hue can increase productivity—such as reading comprehension and physical ability—yet it is a natural appetite suppressant.

**PURPLE:** Purple is the color most associated with royalty. At its lightest (lavender), purple is quiet and meditative; darker purples, such as eggplant, are more sophisticated.

**NEUTRALS:** These hues—beige, taupe, brown, white, gray, and black—have the ability to temper bold hues, providing a sense of balance in a space.

# BRIGHT SPOTS

**IF YOU ARE A COLLECTOR,** surround yourself with treasured items to make work time more enjoyable. Bowling balls, pottery, and globes—in warm and cool colors—create a high-energy setting in this office *opposite*. The blond furniture and light-tone walls and flooring balance the bold accessories.

**VIVID RED "POPS"** off the purple wall in this office niche *left* as an eye-catching focal point. The artwork is painted, prestretched canvas, available in many sizes at crafts and art supply stores. This technique allows you to inexpensively add color that can be repainted on a whim.

**TROPICAL COLORS** and patterns enliven the office *below*; however, the background—soft green walls and midtone wood finishes—retains a restful feel. The trick? The hot-pink accents and floral-motif fabric are used sparingly and sprinkled throughout the space.

# Laundry Rooms

Does tending to the laundry give you the blues? Lift your spirits and turn the mundane task into an enjoyable experience by filling your laundry room with color. The rooms on pages 86–89 prove that this utilitarian space can be fun as well as functional.

## DARKS AND LIGHTS

**IF YOU WANT AN UPSCALE LOOK** in your laundry room, choose rich colors—such as bittersweet, cabernet, plum, or chocolate—sophisticated finishes, and high-quality materials. This laundry *opposite* features rusty red walls and furniture-quality cabinets, which sport a neutral and green distressed finish; the complementary colors (red and green) are harmonized because they are used in equal doses and are tempered by plenty of white (the countertop and floor).

**SUNFLOWER YELLOW ACCENTS** give this space *right* a sunny disposition. The hue is surrounded by white, the dominant color in this scheme, which intensifies the impact of the yellow. To make a similar cheerful stripe motif more serious, eliminate the white in favor of a deeper shade of sunflower.

# Building a Blue Color Scheme

Regardless of the tint or shade, blue promotes rest and relaxation: Watery blues evoke feelings of a lake or seaside getaway, while deep midnight blue welcomes sleep. This versatile hue has the ability to work alone or cool down a too-hot color scheme. But, for all its positive attributes, blue can be chilly on its own, so learning how to use it effectively is important. Here are some tips for creating an all-blue room as well as ideas for successful color-scheme partnerships in the laundry or any space.

TO CREATE AN ALL-BLUE ROOM that appears peaceful, limit the palette to one or two blues, such as in the living room on *page 23*. If you opt for two, use a tint

and a shade of the same hue to harmonize the palette. To prevent the scheme from being too sedate, incorporate patterned textiles and touchable texture, such as in the family room on *page 54*. Neutrals and wood tones work well with blues, but for interest, select accessories in intense or bright blues. Warm up an overly chilly space with elements in brass, terra-cotta, and brick-red hues.

SCHEMES WITH BLUE as a dominant or accent color offer a host of palette possibilities. Combining blue and another hue is an especially smart idea in cold climates, because an all-blue room can be too cool for comfort. For instance, the

kitchen on *page 76* is dominated by blue, but the red and white floor treatment and red accents add warmth. Blue accents can add drama and interest to a space; for example, a blue pillow in the laundry room *above* draws the eye to the bench and window, and a blue painting excites the white living room on *page 25*. Here are a few blue schemes to consider for your home:

Midnight Blue and Gold
Cobalt Blue and Orange
Sky Blue and Grass Green
Powder Blue and Lilac
Cornflower Blue and Yellow
Aqua Blue and Sea-Glass Green
Navy Blue, Flag Red, and Yellow

# WATERY BLUES

**BUTTERCREAM AND WHITE** add subtle color to this laundry room *opposite*. One blue pillow draws the eye to the inviting window seat—and away from the appliances.

**A MIX OF BLUES** lends a nostalgic note to this old-fashioned laundry *left*; graniteware and pewter pitchers accentuate the vintage look. Because the blues—on the floor and window—are separated by expanses of white, the color variety is interesting and charming rather than distracting.

**COOL COLORS TYPICALLY RECEDE,** but this ultramarine blue—with red undertones—visually draws in the walls of this large, multifunctional space *below*. To prevent the deep color from appearing too heavy, it is tempered by planes of white, gray, and stainless steel.

# Resting Spaces

Creating a bedroom or bathroom is relatively easy; creating a place of rest and rejuvenation can be more difficult. As you plan the decorating themes and color schemes for your master, guest, or child's bedroom and your baths, think about the mood and energy level you want the spaces to convey. The bedrooms and baths on pages 90–127 show you myriad options for using color to create a personal haven, from master bedrooms that encourage sweet dreams to kids' rooms that inspire creativity with their vivid schemes.

**LUXURIOUS BLUE AND CHOCOLATE BROWN** converge for an elegant bedroom *opposite*. The rich wood tones keep the scheme warm, while cheery yellow accents—the flowers on the bedside table and in the oil paintings—perk up the blue.

# Master Suites

Close your eyes and envision your dream getaway. Whether it is a luxury resort on a remote island or a quaint bed-and-breakfast, you can capture that feeling in your master suite by selecting the right colors, furnishings, and textures. In the inspiring spaces on the following pages, we'll show you how to make every day feel like a vacation.

## CHOCOLATE PASSION

**IF YOU WANT TO CREATE A ROMANTIC RETREAT**—but you don't care for lacy linens and canopy beds—follow the cues in this passionate master suite *opposite* and *right*. Red, the color of passion, combines with light and dark chocolate for a warm, sensual feel; both the bedroom and bath have been treated to the same colors and intensities for continuity. Soothing textures—the suede and napped throw pillows and ribbed coverlet in the bedroom and the velvety towels and robe in the bathroom—are a treat for the senses.

**COOL WHITE AND SHINY CHROME ACCENTS** in the bath *right* reduce the heat of the warm palette.

# SUMMER GARDEN

**INSPIRED BY A COLLECTION** of botanical prints *below*, this master suite *opposite* wears the soft pinks, rosy reds, and greens of a late-summer garden. The mix of patterns—stripes and florals that share a common palette—distressed furnishings with ornate details, and heavy doses of white combine for a soothing retreat that feels expansive. The dark upholstered chair anchors the light colors.

**THE ARRANGEMENT** of the sitting area table *below* in this suite is formal—the prints and lamps are in perfect symmetry—but the soft colors and distressed table make the setting more relaxed.

# Use Pattern and Texture to Create Interest

Interiors that mix color, pattern, and texture entertain the eye. An interplay of elements is especially important in spaces that sport a neutral or monochromatic scheme, such as the bedroom shown here: Generally, the less color used, the greater the need for pattern and texture to add visual interest. Textural contrast is easy to achieve in a bedroom—where numerous textiles are often used—and you can use the same principles to tempt the senses in any room of the home. Here are some popular options:

### EMBELLISHMENTS
Bows or ties
Buttons
Cording or piping
Fringe
Gathers
Medallions
Pleats
Ruffles
Scallops
Tassels

### HANDCRAFTED ITEMS
Appliqué
Embroidery
Hooked rugs
Knitted throws
Quilts
Tapestries

### PATTERNED FABRICS
Checks
Florals
Geometric prints
Houndstooth
Paisley
Plaid
Tone-on-tone

### TEXTURED FABRICS
Chenille
Jacquard
Linen
Machine embroidery
Mohair
Plush or faux fur
Raised tone-on-tone
Raw silk
Velvet
Wool

# SPRING GREENS

**THIS MONOCHROMATIC SUITE** *opposite*, *right*, and *below* is enlivened by a mix of interesting patterns—checks and a variety of florals—and textures. Because all the fabrics share the same palette, the look is harmonized, not busy.

**WHITE TRIM AND ACCENTS,** as well as dark-tone wood furnishings—which ground the airy color scheme *below*—unify the bedroom, sitting area, and bath (not shown). Using the same color of trim throughout a master suite is an easy way to create visual continuity.

**DRESSMAKER DETAILS** on the window treatments and pillows *right* and the bedding *opposite* enhance the upscale feel of this suite.

# BLUE HEAVEN

**CREATE HARMONY** and a restful environment by splashing all the walls in a master suite with pale blue. The blue in this suite *below* and *opposite* creates continuity throughout the open plan; the white furnishings continue the airy feel. The contrasting black-tile facade of the fireplace, which divides the space into a bedroom and sitting area, makes the fireplace an instant focal point.

**METAL ACCENTS** finish a room much like a stunning silver necklace does a little black dress. Generally, golden-hue metals work best with warm tones, while silver-tone metals complement cool tones. The tray *right* is one of many silver accents in this room. By featuring one metal throughout this large space, the sense of color continuity is enhanced.

**SHOTS OF WARM COLOR** *below*—the oranges, bright book spine, and dollops of warm hues in the framed prints—add some necessary heat to this master suite.

# WHISPERS OF COLOR

**PALE YELLOW AND BLUE** offer quiet hints of color in this soothing white-dominant bedroom *below* and *right*. The bed is the focal point of this space; its graceful lines and carved details are emphasized because the recessed areas are painted in a darker hue. To create a restful bedroom similar to this, paint your wood furniture a solid, neutral color; this will eliminate the visual excitement of wood graining.

**WARM COLORS TYPICALLY ENERGIZE** an all-white room, but if you add gray to the hue, the effect can be peaceful rather than overbearing. All the grayed-yellow accents in this suite *opposite* are of the same intensity, creating a relaxed but upbeat look. For a more invigorating environment, use yellows of various intensities.

# Connect Spaces with Color

Here are some foolproof ways to use color to link rooms, such as a master bedroom, bathroom, and closet, or other areas that relate to one another, to create a sense of continuity.

LIMIT THE PALETTE used within the spaces. Select two or three colors that work well together and use them in varying amounts in each of the rooms. For example, the white bedroom *above* has yellow draperies and accents, but the adjoining bathroom may shift to yellow walls and white accents. A more complex and broader selection of colors may be developed for a whole-house color palette. For example, the multicolor living room shown on *page 14* may represent all of the colors used within the home. Rather than repeating the entire palette in every room, which would become monotonous, subsequent spaces such as the dining room may feature only one or two of the hues.

THREAD A FAVORITE COLOR throughout the spaces. For instance, a neutral-palette room decorated in brown, taupe, and off-white—such as the living room on *page 21*—could have one accent color, such as the vivid pink. The same pink could be used in other connecting rooms to forge a visual link.

FLOORS CAN play an important role in creating a sense of continuity; you can either use the same type and color of flooring throughout the open area or select different materials to delineate functional areas (for instance, use carpeting in the bedroom and tile in the connecting bath). If you choose the latter, select flooring in similar colors and intensities to retain visual continuity.

SELECT THE SAME TRIM COLOR for the space, whether it's a wood stain or paint color, to unify the area. Rooms that connect, such as the bedroom and bath of a master suite, can be different from the rest of the home; just match the outside of the hall door to the other doors to make a smooth transition between the spaces.

# Guest Rooms

Secondary bedrooms in today's households often serve visiting family members and out-of-town guests. In some cases, the rooms are used infrequently; sometimes they play host regularly. Either way, these bedrooms need to be friendly, nurturing, and relaxing spaces. Use the color lessons on the following pages to help you decorate the guest bedrooms in your home.

## A TOUCH OF PINK

**SOFT PINK HAS A QUIETING EFFECT,** making it a nice choice for guest rooms, but pink can make a space look too feminine. As an antidote in your guest room, use pink as an accent. Green and white dominate the guest room *opposite*, and pink plays a supporting, romantic role; the graphic wall treatment further offsets the effects of the pretty hue.

**AN INTENSE PINK**—rather than a powder-puff pink, which would be the true complement of the cucumber green in this guest space *right*—adds punch when it's used as an accent. The deeper pink is also more gender-neutral than the lighter tint, making it appealing to male guests.

# Add Hospitality with Color

Whether you entertain overnight guests frequently or have visitors only on occasion, the primary goal for a dedicated guest room is to create a welcoming environment.

WHEN CHOOSING A PALETTE and decorating scheme for a guest room, you can either continue the style you've chosen for the rest of your home or select a scheme and decor that are slightly different for added interest.

FOR A SENSE OF UNITY, you can connect the room to the other spaces in your home without duplicating the colors exactly: Use lighter or darker or brighter or duller variations, or establish a neutral background and use the chosen color(s) as an accent. (See *page 101* for tips on how to create color continuity within your home.)

THE BEACH HOUSE GUEST ROOM shown on *page 107 bottom* is a good example of maintaining style continuity in a lighter, softer palette. While the public areas on the first floor of the home sport bright yellow and blue, the second floor and this guest room feature calming pastels. Elements used on both levels, such as wicker or painted-wood furniture and small floral prints, provide style continuity for the home.

IF VARIETY is appealing to you, go for it! To forge a visual link between the space and the rest of the home—even if the overall style is different—you can still opt for the same color of trim or carry one color from an adjoining room into the guest space to make the transition less jarring.

REGARDLESS OF YOUR CHOICE, keep in mind that the aim is to create a restful space for a guest retreat. As such, avoid intense palettes—such as pairing strong red and bold blue—that could be unsettling. Peruse the dedicated guest rooms in this section and the master suites on *pages 92–101* for color schemes and decorating ideas that your guests are sure to love.

# BOLD HUES

**TONE DOWN** the boisterous personality of a bright or saturated hue in a guest room by using black or dark-hue furnishings. The orange wall color in this bedroom *opposite* is cheerful; the sophisticated, dark furnishings ground the room.

**CHOOSE A NEUTRAL FOUNDATION** for a guest room to make it easier to update the space with textiles and accessories for each season or for guests with different tastes. For instance, the space *right* is sleek and chic because of the graphic yellow-green accents; you could eliminate that hue and pair the gray backdrop with a warm pink or orange for a completely different look.

**DREAMY TURQUOISE BLUE** *below* is intense, but lots of white balances the bold hue. The dark floor grounds the scheme; the orange flowers add a shot of warm color.

105

# SERENE SPACES

**CREATE A ZEN–LIKE ENVIRONMENT** by choosing a nature-inspired palette for a guest room. In the space *opposite*, the colors, low-slung furnishings, and minimal, modern accessories encourage peace. Wrapping the lower third of the walls with deep chocolate brown puts the focus on the bed by enveloping it with color.

**ANOTHER WAY TO ENSURE THE BED** takes center stage in any bedroom—be it a master bedroom, guest room, or kid's space—is to frame the furnishing with a color that is deeper than the rest of the walls. In this guest room *right*, the bed sits in a blue-painted niche; the rest of the walls are painted a soft white, keeping the emphasis on the bed. The quiet color scheme invites rest.

**WHITE EVOKES FEELINGS** of peace in this seaside beach home *below*. This white bedroom seems open and airy because the eye is free to roam. The aged green chair and bedspreads and the rose-color pillow and flowers introduce a hint of contemporary color; this limited use of color doesn't detract from the lazy-day ambiance.

# Kids' Rooms

The most creative and lighthearted place in a home should be where the children play and sleep. Use color to dress kids' rooms to suit their preferences and yours. Color possibilities are as unlimited as a child's imagination. The rooms on the following pages show all the options, from restful green and pink to perky orange and aqua. Use the color lessons from these fun spaces to create a treasured room for your own child.

## TWIST ON LIME

**AGELESS COLOR SCHEMES,** such as the green and pink palette in this bedroom *opposite*, can be used through the years because they are appealing to kids of all ages, from early elementary age to college age. To create a room that grows with your child, select classic color mixes that stay in style, such as red, white, and blue, or navy and gold.

**PAINT THE BED** with a fun design to add the playfulness your child desires. The pattern on this bed *right* was easily created with stamps and freehand designs. A simple treatment such as this can serve a variety of ages and can easily be covered—with a coat of primer and paint—when your child's interests or color choices change.

# HOT COLORS

**A DYNAMIC MULTICOLOR RUG** *opposite* provides the color inspiration for this bedroom. A single patterned item, such as a rug, bedding, or wallpaper, can guide the color selection for the other elements in the room and give the space continuity. In this case, the rug and wall-hung art connect all the solid blocks of color used throughout the space.

**AS WITH ANY ROOM,** creating a neutral background allows you to change accessories—and add any color to the mix—on a whim. In the bedroom *below,* if the young occupant tires of the bright yellows, greens, and pinks, those elements can be removed without disrupting the shell of the room (the neutral-hue bed, shelving, and flooring).

# Plan Color to Grow with Your Child

Growing up is hard to do if you're a 10-year-old living in a 2-year-old's room. When it comes to planning a child's bedroom, keeping up with his or her ever-maturing body, mind, and tastes can be difficult—not to mention expensive. Follow these tips to create a color- and wallet-friendly space that will grow with your child.

READY-MADE BEDDING AND WINDOW TREATMENTS featuring the latest cartoon character or superhero can go out of style fast. To avoid replacing these often-expensive items on a regular basis, choose solid-color bedding you can mix and match. If your child is begging for a cartoon-theme element in his or her

room, purchase inexpensive items, such as pillows and lampshades. Also, buy the best-quality bedding and textiles you can afford: Sheets with a high thread count will feel better and wear longer, saving money in the long run.

EASY-TO-WASH WALLPAPER can be an asset in a child's room, but removing and hanging wallpaper can be a chore. Instead, paint the walls with washable, cleanable formulations in solid colors or easy-to-create geometric patterns, such as playful wide stripes. Establishing a simple foundation makes it easier to change the furnishings and accessories as tastes and interests change.

KIDS' STUFF IS COLORFUL and can offer interest to their rooms. Incorporate everyday items, such as toys and books, into the color scheme. Paint wooden or metal display shelves with neutral colors and change only the accessories as the child matures.

USE ART AND BULLETIN BOARDS for a quick dose of color. Frame artwork or posters in colorful borders: Select picture frames with removable backs in neutrals or a color children won't tire of so the frames can be reused with fresh art. Or cover a bulletin board with paint or fabric to work with any scheme (you can quickly update the look with a new color or fabric whenever the mood strikes).

# PEACEFUL DREAMS

**IF YOUR CHILD** has an affinity for collections, use them to draw color inspiration. The art and antiques in this teenager's room *opposite* directed the wall and trim colors; the cool hues are restful and allow the historical pieces to take center stage.

**IT'S OBVIOUS** what the most important feature of this bedroom *right* is. Positioned against a creamy yellow and white background, the bed—with its colorful canopy and vivid, patterned bedding—is firmly established as the focal point. The multicolor accessories, which are spread throughout the space, add whimsy.

**SCHEMES OF GREEN, YELLOW, AND PINK** can often be too sweet, but the white bedding, window sheers, and canopy soften the impact of these midtone hues in the bedroom *below*.

# WATERWORKS

**COOL BLUE AND GREEN** create a harmonious scheme in this sea- and surf-theme bedroom *below*. Red, the complement of green, adds visual punch; orange, the complement of blue, would have a similar energizing effect on the space.

**PAINTED WHITE TRIM** makes a pastel palette clean and bright. The window seat in a child's room *right* is washed in cool pastel hues (blue, green, and lilac); the white accents neutralize the chilly scheme. If your child's room needs color relief but the room doesn't have architectural details such as molding or built-ins, incorporate white furnishings or artwork with white frames and mats.

**BOLD PATTERNS** can work for a child's room; just ensure all the patterns share a common palette, as do the florals and checks in this teenage girl's bedroom *opposite*. Planes of solid color—the light-color flooring, green table, and white bedding—tone down the vivid scheme.

# Age Influences Color Preferences

Have you ever wondered why your child selects certain crayon colors or prefers one shirt over another based solely on color? Have you and your child struggled to agree on one paint color over another for his or her room? If so, the answer may be simple: Children see color differently than adults.

OBVIOUSLY, CHILDREN'S eyes are younger and have not changed due to the aging process. Consequently, their eyes absorb 10 percent of the blue light that passes through their lenses. Compare this to the larger amount of blue light that adult eyes absorb: 85 percent. (This

is due to fluids in the lenses yellowing with age.) The result is many adults prefer blue, while kids most often choose yellow. Adults have shown that after blue, they prefer red, green, white, pink, violet, and orange. Kids followed their favored yellow with white, pink, red, orange, blue, green, and violet.

BUT THERE ARE ALWAYS exceptions. Experience can also play a role in color associations, which influence preferences. For example, adults have a broader range of experiences—and may have been exposed to travel, art, or other factors—and they may be drawn to colors

that elicit pleasant thoughts or memories. Conversely, a child's limited range of experience—brightly colored cartoon characters or the bold schemes of sports teams—likely influences his or her preferences.

WHATEVER YOUR CHILD'S PREFERENCES, try to incorporate the colors into his or her room. Play up the ones you agree on and that work with the rest of the coloring in the home. Use these for wall, flooring, and permanent window coverings, such as blinds. Use the other hues for items that can easily be changed.

# LILAC BLOOMS

**VISUALLY LOWER A HIGH CEILING** in a child's room by positioning molding on the wall several inches from the ceiling line. Paint the area above the molding a deep color that contrasts with the rest of the wall color to further the illusion, as was done in this teenage girl's room *right*. A combination of warm and cool hues—and seaside accessories—evokes memories of sunny days at the beach.

**LILAC, BLUE, AND RED** combine for an analogous palette in this bedroom *below*. Because these are warm colors (blue and lilac are cool colors, but the hues in this space have red undertones that add warmth), they are energetic and playful when combined. Using white furniture, draperies, and accents prevents this heated scheme from overpowering the space.

# Bathrooms

With the development of more durable, washable paints and wallpapers—along with an expanded offering of stylish bath products, from flooring and tiles to textiles—making your bathroom a haven that reflects your personality is easier than ever. The baths on pages 118–127 prove that any hue, from warm reds to cool blues and calming neutrals, can be used successfully in a bath.

## TAMING RED

**RED WALLS** make this bath *opposite* feel cozy and inviting. The art, shelving with books, and substantial furnishings take the edge off the bold hue, making it appropriate for a bath. When choosing a wall color for your bath, keep in mind that much of the color may be concealed behind wall-hung elements, such as mirrors, artwork, and cabinets.

**RUSTY-RED ACCENTS** add warmth to the pale green aged-stucco finish in this bath *right*. The draped window treatments complement the rounded edges (such as the curvy sink and mirror frames), warm-tone woods, and metal finishes used throughout the space. Red towels, rugs, or flowers would have a similar effect.

# COLOR INJECTION

**BOLD BLOCKS OF COLOR** appear orderly in this bath *opposite*, thanks to wide molding on the walls and ceiling and the hefty mirror frame, which break up the expanses of color. You can use existing architecture to "frame" areas of color or install trim, which is readily available in many widths at home centers.

**WAKE UP SLEEPYHEADS** with color. The hot pink in this bathroom *below* is sure to energize the body and mind. Blue accents—in the rug and shower curtain and the towels—cool down the bright hue. Baths are ideal places in which to experiment with bold hues; they are typically small spaces, and we spend less time in our baths than other rooms of the home.

**FLOWER-MOTIF** fabric inspired the wall color in this bath *right*. Because bright yellow can be irritating to some eyes, choose a grayed yellow, such as this sunflower hue.

**SOFT GREEN** promotes relaxation in this eclectic bath *left*. The chrome accents and graphic pink rug lend an urban vibe, while the claw-foot tub speaks to a country aesthetic. The green walls and accents (towels and the bird illustration) bring harmony to the disparate elements.

**GREEN TILES** with a yellow undertone set a quiet backdrop for the main feature in this bath *below*: the hammered-metal mirror frame. The white elements bring further emphasis to the mirror.

**GREEN DOMINATES** this country-inspired bath *opposite*. The green-painted beaded board on the lower portion of the walls and the black countertop ground the white-printed wallpaper that soars to the ceiling.

# GREEN SCHEMES

# Pairing Color with Design Styles

Whatever your bathroom's style, from modern to traditional, most are best supported by the right color. Here are a few color choices for several styles.

**Mid-Century Modern:** Colors most often associated with this style include soft blue, aqua, and pink; black or chrome are common accents. Other colors that may also work are those seen in period pottery, as shown on *page 125*.

**Romantic Country:** Imagine the colors of a blooming flower garden—from yellow daisies to purple lilacs and bluebells to strawberry-red roses—and you're on the right track, as long as the colors are softened with plenty of white. Most often

the hues are tints, such as pastels. If you opt for bolder versions of these colors, use them as accents with a large percentage of white, cream, or a neutral.

**Contemporary:** Creating drama through color is an important goal for this aesthetic. Often bold color pairings or deep-to-light color contrasts (see the deep chocolate and white hallway on *page 140*) work well for a contemporary look.

**Traditional:** Hunt-club colors—deep green, cabernet, navy, and plum—are the most obvious, but updated traditional looks incorporate a host of preppy brights, such as sunny yellow, azalea pink, and apple green.

**Arts and Crafts:** Organic colors, such as yellow-green, shown *opposite right*, sage green, yellow-gold, and rusty red are a few colors that work to express this style.

**Old-World Tuscan:** Aged-stucco colors, including terra-cotta, faded gold, and washed-out apricot, make a nice backdrop for this style (see *page 119*).

**Urban Casual:** Crisp to grayed greens and blues and an abundant selection of neutrals provide a quiet foundation for rich wood tones or black furniture.

**Country French:** The colors of Provençe include vivid blue, golden yellow, poppy red, burnt orange, and green.

# BLUE MOODS

**POWDER BLUE AND WHITE** have a calming effect in this charming bath *below*. The quiet blue color is positioned between the architectural elements; the hue recedes to give the trim importance, but it flows from wall to wall, visually enlarging the space. Silver accents complement the cool palette.

**HIGH-CONTRAST PAIRS**—such as black and white—can be overly serious, but incorporating one colored element can shift the mood. This bath *right* is a case in point: The blue frosted-glass shower door takes the overall look from formal to peaceful.

**IF YOU CRAVE A BATH** that washes away stress, select a Zen-like palette of browns and greens. The bath *opposite* features a Mother Nature-inspired color scheme, organic shapes (such as the pottery), and natural materials.

# SPA WHITE

**USE COLOR SPARINGLY** for a peaceful bath. The large green plant in this bath *right* invigorates the neutral-dominant palette.

**THOUGH WHITE** is the most popular color for bath fixtures, you can play up a focal-point tub with an unexpected splash of color. A jolt of warm color is introduced in this light, airy bath *below*, compliments of a brown-painted claw-foot tub. The warm wood tones of the door and freestanding furnishings make the tub blend seamlessly with the rest of the bath.

**IF THE CLEAN, CRISP APPEARANCE** of an all-white bath appeals to you, use a wide range of whites—from warm to cool—and abundant textural elements to add interest. The bath *opposite* is far from sedate, with its mix of tile, beaded board, and soft terry towels. The dark chair, multicolor rug, and pink flowers add warmth to the space.

# Add Color without Commitment

If you are ready to add color to your bath—or any room of the home—but you don't want to commit to a new wall or flooring color, consider these ideas. Any of these options are easy to replace with the change of the season or whenever the mood strikes.

**PRIME AND PAINT** inexpensive mirror and picture frames for a splash of wall-hung color. Use the frames to display prints or photographs.

**BATHS CAN BE MADE** more comfortable with textiles—beyond window treatments. If space allows, bring a chair into your bath and place a colorful cushion or pillow made of a water-friendly fabric on the chair. Tubs, even without showers, benefit from a drapery hung from the ceiling. Screw eye-hooks into the ceiling and hook or tie ready-made panels to divide the space and add instant color. And, of course, colorful towels can be displayed on hooks or towel bars, or can be rolled and stored in a large woven basket.

**IF YOU HAVE A COLLECTION** of pottery, dishware, enamelware, or vases, display it to add shots of color to your bath and make the space feel more personal. Or, create displays on your countertop or a windowsill with natural materials, such as flowers and leaves.

**RUGS** offer an easy way to colorize a space. You can purchase ready-made rugs or make your own by painting an artist's canvas for a floorcloth (coat with polyacrylic for durability). Or, use precut stencils or foam stamps and crafts paint to add a colorful design to a sisal rug.

**PLANTS BRING LIFE** to all rooms; in the bath, they also soften the hard edges of tiled surfaces. Tropical plants that love moisture are best. They can be found in a variety of leafy greens; some have the potential to provide colorful flowers.

**IF YOU HAVE** space for a wall-hung or freestanding shelf, use books to introduce color, as shown in the bath on *page 118*.

# Transition Spaces

The old adage "getting there is half the fun" doesn't apply solely to world travel or life experiences: This can also describe the "transition" spaces in your home that lead you from one room to the next. That doesn't mean your stairways and hallways need to be bright or wildly decorated; instead, they should take you and guests on a pleasant journey through your home. The spaces on pages 128–141 show you how to use color to encourage traffic flow and provide a visual link between rooms.

**USE COLOR** to make a grand entrance: The cornflower blue and red surrounding this staircase *opposite* are similar in intensity. The voluminous ceiling feels less cavernous because of the visual weight of the blue and the vibration between the colors.

# Staircases

There is something intrinsically romantic about a staircase. This architectural feature seems to promise happiness, grand entries, and, at times, even a dramatic exit (think *Gone with the Wind* and other favorite movies). In both the movies and real life, staircases have been the gracious backdrop for family photos, revealed a plethora of prom dresses and tuxes, and introduced a bevy of brides. The stairways on the following pages will inspire you to use color to ensure a heavenly flight.

## NATURALLY GREAT

**EXTEND THE LIVING ROOM COLOR** up a stairwell to enlarge the area and encourage color flow to rooms upstairs. This shade of green *opposite* is a soothing nature-inspired backdrop for the warm-tone flooring and furnishings. To forge a visual link between this color and the rest of the home, rooms connecting to the hallway could incorporate the green as an accent.

# LIGHT RISE

**USE A DEEP COLOR** to fill wide-open spaces. Warm mustard yellow *opposite* provides depth to this sweeping staircase; the clean expanse of rich color plays up the slender spindles of the balustrade. The bold red vase vibrates against the greenish hue.

**COLOR CAN PERFORM** as a visual palette cleanser in a stairway, giving the eyes and senses a break between rooms with disparate color schemes. The refreshing green *below* complements the old-world-inspired staircase and offers a clean break between the sitting area with berry-color accents and the dusky lavender hallway upstairs (not shown).

**DRAW YOUR EYE UP A STAIRCASE** by using the same color on the walls and a carpet runner. The yellow of the walls and runner *right*—combined with the raised-panel wall treatment and dark stair rail—lead the gaze upward.

# TRUE BLUE

**USING BLOCKS OF COLORS**—rather than a single color— makes a large staircase interesting. This stairwell *left* (also shown on *page 128*) includes blue, red, and green sections. A treatment such as this works best for transition areas with architectural dividers, such as corners or short walls, which contain the colors.

**IF YOUR STAIRCASE** lacks architectural details, use a graphic paint treatment to add interest, such as the pale blue and white stripes *below*.

**SUNNY YELLOW AND COOL OCEAN BLUE** are the perfect combination for beach house stairs *opposite*. Only the risers are painted to prevent the deep blue color from overpowering the space.

# Creating Successful Transitions

Stairways and hallways are meant to efficiently transport people from one space to the next. As such, they can be tricky to decorate because they shouldn't include physical barriers, should provide "visual activity" to keep passersby entertained, and they "touch" so many rooms of the home. Here are some ideas for creating transition spaces that complement the surrounding spaces and serve their intended function.

FORGE A CONNECTION between the transition space and adjoining rooms by lining the walls with objects that include colors from the spaces. Art, photos, quilts, and plates are just a few options. For example, the stairway on *page 133*

*left* features small oil paintings of animals. The colors in the art and even the frames are reminiscent of the colors and intensities used in the rooms the space connects.

ENCOURAGE MOVEMENT THROUGH THE SPACE by incorporating elements that repeat in a slow, even manner. For example, a series of evenly spaced lithographs in a hallway creates a visual pattern that can influence the pace at which people walk. The large painting on *page 138*, for example, adds color without distraction.

TO KEEP A CLEAR PATH, use small-scale furniture in hallways. For instance,

a tall, skinny piece can make a tight space feel larger because it doesn't take up much floor space. If seating is needed, shallow-depth or small-scale benches, such as the one in the hallway on *page 136*, are the perfect solution for a free-flowing space. Similarly, rather than placing tables in a hall, hang a shelf on which you can display items to make the walk more interesting.

GOOD LIGHTING IS CRITICAL for hallways and stairways to ensure safety. Lighting has the added bonus of creating drama and highlighting important features, such as artwork. Incorporate mirrors to increase the light and make a small space appear bigger.

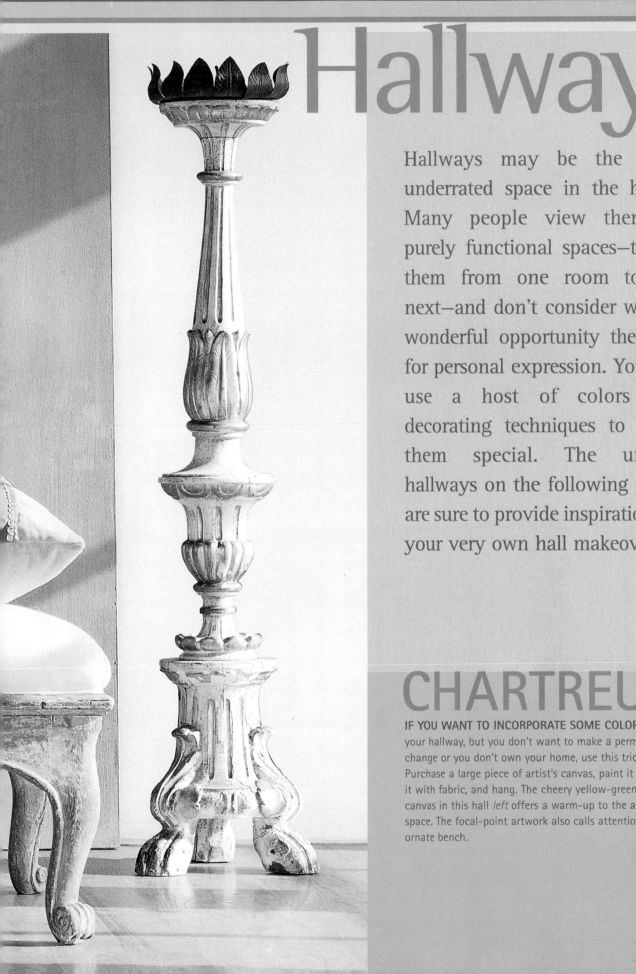

# Hallways

Hallways may be the most underrated space in the home: Many people view them as purely functional spaces–to get them from one room to the next–and don't consider what a wonderful opportunity they are for personal expression. You can use a host of colors and decorating techniques to make them special. The unique hallways on the following pages are sure to provide inspiration for your very own hall makeover.

## CHARTREUSE

**IF YOU WANT TO INCORPORATE SOME COLOR** into your hallway, but you don't want to make a permanent change or you don't own your home, use this trick: Purchase a large piece of artist's canvas, paint it or cover it with fabric, and hang. The cheery yellow-green-painted canvas in this hall *left* offers a warm-up to the all-white space. The focal-point artwork also calls attention to the ornate bench.

# OLD BLUES

**HALLWAYS ARE IDEAL PLACES** in which to hang paintings or display collections because they offer an expanse of uninterrupted wall space. The hallway *opposite* allows those passing through to escape into the painting, the most colorful element in the neutral space.

**PRETTY PALE BLUE,** distressed wood, and seaside accessories combine for a calm display in this hall *right*. The mix of items and textures makes the collection interesting to view from many angles.

**TINTS OF COLORS,** such as the light blue in the hallway *below*, and white reflect light, making a small area feel more spacious.

# NEUTRAL ZONE

**DARK BROWN FACES OFF WITH WHITE** *left.* Usually, a dark color will make a small space feel claustrophobic, but here the interplay of dark and light doesn't make the hallway feel closed in. Lighting—natural and artificial—also makes the space feel airy.

**LIGHT AND MIDTONE COLORS** highlight architectural details better than dark hues, as this hallway *right* proves. The reason? Lighter colors, such as this tan, emphasize the natural shadows of the arches, flutes, and cove molding, making the details "pop" off the shadowed, recessed areas.

## Common Names for Color Groups

Colors that share common traits are often clustered into groups. The following are some popular identifiers.

**PASTELS:** Technically referred to as tints, pastels are base colors to which white has been added. The greater the amount of white, the paler the color. Pastels visually move away, or retreat, from the eye and make rooms feel airy and light (see the dining room on *page 42* as an example). Pastels include baby pink, powder blue, peach, and mint green.

**NEUTRALS:** These are technically "noncolors," ranging from white to black and off-white to the deepest chocolate. Neutrals also encompass the very palest

form of color, such as white with the slightest hint of blue or green. Names of neutrals include cocoa, charcoal, coffee, and cream (see *pages 20* and *21* for living rooms that use these hues).

**MIDTONES:** These colors lie on both sides of a base color. Gray makes them deeper than pastels and more muted than brights. Colors include apricot, dusty lavender, and sage green (see the sage green bedroom on *pages 96* and *97*).

**DARKS OR DEEP TONES:** These hues occur when black or gray is added to a base color; they are also called shades. These colors make walls advance and cause a room to feel smaller and cozier

(see the home theater on *page 66*). Deep tones include plum, navy blue, hunter green, cabernet, and burgundy.

**BRIGHTS:** These are colors with high intensity and a high level of saturation; this commonly includes any color that is especially bold. These are the colors that children often love, such as fire-engine red, lemon yellow, hot pink, and bright blue (see the child's room on *page 114*).

**NEONS:** Adapted from neon-gaslight colors, these colors are extremely bright. At times called electric or fluorescent, neon hues are best used in very small amounts or when contrasted with natural tones (see the living room on *page 12*).

# INDEX